# Young
# Davy Crockett

### Frontier Pioneer

A Troll First-Start® Biography

*by Eric Carpenter*
*illustrated by Jenny Williams*

## Troll Associates

*Library of Congress Cataloging-in-Publication Data*

Carpenter, Eric.
    Young Davy Crockett: frontier pioneer / by Eric Carpenter;
illustrated by Jenny Williams.
      p.     cm.— (A Troll first-start biography)
    ISBN 0-8167-3758-4 (lib. bdg.)    ISBN 0-8167-3759-2 (pbk.)
     1. Crockett, Davy, 1786-1836—Juvenile literature.    2. Pioneers—
Tennessee—Biography—Juvenile literature.   3. Tennessee—
Biography—Juvenile literature.   4. Legislators—United States—
Biography—Juvenile literature.   5. United States.   Congress.
House—Biography—Juvenile literature.   I. Williams, Jenny,
ill.  II. Title.  III. Series.
F436.C95C37   1996
976.804'092—dc20
  [B]                                      95-7598

Davy Crockett was a hero of the American frontier.

He was born in Tennessee in 1786. Davy
lived with his family in a log cabin in the
wilderness.

Pioneers like the Crocketts had to work
hard just to make sure they had enough
food and a warm place to sleep.

When Davy was only 6 years old, his uncle, Joseph Hawkins, taught him to hunt. They spent many hours in the woods tracking deer, bears, and other animals.

Davy was too young to hunt on his own,
but he loved hunting with Uncle Joe.
Davy was lucky to have such a good
woodsman teaching him.

When Davy was almost 8 years old, his family moved and had to build a new home. Since Davy was too young to help, he asked if he could go hunting.

Davy's father decided he was old enough
to hunt by himself. But he gave Davy only
one bullet a day, because bullets were so
expensive!

At first Davy did not have much luck.
But he quickly learned to be careful
and patient.

10

Before long, Davy was able to bring home
meat for his family almost every day.

Life was not easy for the Crockett family.
In the spring, heavy rains fell and the
creek flooded. Their home was destroyed.

The Crocketts moved to an inn.
All the Crocketts had jobs to do.
Davy was the family's hunter.

One day, a man staying at the inn asked
Davy's parents if Davy could help him
bring his cattle from Tennessee to Virginia.

Davy enjoyed the trip. When he reached
Virginia, Davy decided to stay awhile.

15

But after a few weeks, Davy went back to
Tennessee and his family. Davy was happy
to be home, and his family was happy to
see him again.

When Davy was 13, he went to school for the first time. Davy was going to learn to read and write.

Pioneer children did not always get to go to school. And the schools were very simple. They had very few books, and students practiced their writing on wooden boards with pieces of charcoal.

Four days after he started school, Davy
got into a fight. He knew he would get into
trouble for fighting.

He decided to run away.

Once again, Davy found work taking cattle to Virginia. Then he worked at many different jobs. Davy stayed away from home for almost three years.

When he did go home, his family was happy and surprised.

Davy was happy to be home again. He even got another chance to go to school.

Davy worked on a farm owned by a local schoolteacher. Instead of money, the teacher paid Davy with food, a place to live, and schooling. He taught Davy to read, write, and do arithmetic.

Getting an education was the best payment Davy could ask for! He needed to know how to read and write if he wanted to do important things in his life.

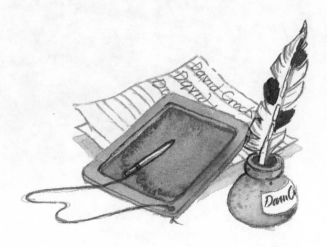

There are many legends about Davy Crockett. A legend is a popular story that is told over and over again. The stories are not always true.

One legend says that Davy was such a good hunter, he killed over 100 bears in one year. Another says that Davy tamed a giant alligator.

But some stories about Davy are true. He was an important man in American history. He became a United States Congressman!

Most of all, Davy Crockett fought for what he believed in. He believed in freedom.

In 1836, Davy went to help Texas gain its independence from Mexico.

Davy joined other men who were fighting for freedom. In San Antonio, the fighting was heavy. Davy and the others retreated to the Alamo, a mission fort.

Davy and the others fought hard for two
weeks. But they did not win.

Davy Crockett died at the Alamo.
But in time Texas won its freedom.

Although there are many legends about Davy,
his real life was filled with exciting adventures.